Play That Thing!

Keith Gaines

OXFORD
UNIVERSITY PRESS

OXFORD
UNIVERSITY PRESS

Great Clarendon Street, Oxford OX2 6DP

Oxford University Press is a department of the University of Oxford.
It furthers the University's objective of excellence in research, scholarship,
and education by publishing worldwide in

Oxford New York

Auckland Cape Town Dar es Salaam Hong Kong Karachi
Kuala Lumpur Madrid Melbourne Mexico City Nairobi
New Delhi Shanghai Taipei Toronto

With offices in

Argentina Austria Brazil Chile Czech Republic France Greece
Guatemala Hungary Italy Japan Poland Portugal Singapore
South Korea Switzerland Thailand Turkey Ukraine Vietnam

with an associated company in Berlin

Oxford is a registered trade mark of Oxford University Press
in the UK and in certain other countries

British Library Cataloguing in Publication Data

Data available

ISBN 0 19 917522 5

10 9 8 7 6 5 4 3

Inspection Pack (nine different titles)
ISBN-13:978-0-19-917524-6
ISBN-10:0-19-917524-1

Acknowledgements

The publishers would like to thank the following for permission to use copyright material:

AKG Photo: p 15; The Art Archive/Lucien Biton Collection, Paris/Dagli Orti: p 9 (*top*); Bridgeman Art
Library/A Concert by Lorenzo Costa (National Gallery, London): p 21, /Garton Orme at the Spinet by
Jonathan Richardson (Holburne Museum and Crafts Study Centre, Bath): p 23 (*top*); Corbis/Lightstone: p 8
(*bottom left*); Hutchison Library/A. Clark: pp 1, 10 (*centre left*), Hutchison Library/J. Von Puttkamer: p 6 (*top
left*); John Hornby Skewes: pp 7 (*bottom left*), 11 (*top*), 17 (*bottom*), 32; Lebrecht Collection/J. Highet: p 11
(*bottom*), Lebrecht Collection/Norman Lebrecht: p 14 (*left*), /P. Kayukwa: p 18 (*bottom*), Lebrecht Collection
/Chris Stock: p 20, Lebrecht Collection/Wladimir Polak: p 24 (*bottom*), Lebrecht Collection/archive: p 28
(*top*); Mary Evans Picture Library: pp 4 (*bottom*), 13 (*top*); Museum of Welsh Life: p 24 (*top*); Pictor
International: pp 7 (*top right*), 7 (*bottom right*); Popperfoto: p 16 (*bottom*); Redferns/J. M. International: p 27,
Redferns/Mick Hutson: p 28 (*bottom*); Still Pictures/Ron Giling: p 4 (top); Topham Picturepoint: p 5 (*bottom*),
/James Marshall/The Image Works: p 10 (*top right*), /The Image Works: p 13 (*bottom*); John Walmsley (with
thanks to Cranleigh Prep School, Cranleigh, and St Peter's RC Comprehensive School, Merrow): pp 6
(*bottom left*), 6 (*right*), 9 (*bottom*), 10 (*bottom right*), 16 (*top*), 22, 23 (*bottom*), 29 and back cover; Werner
Forman Archive/British Museum: p 8 (*bottom right*).

Illustrations by Francis Bacon: pp 12, 30, 31; Bill Donohoe: pp 3, 5 (*top*), 8 (*top*), 14 (*right*), 17 (*top*), 18 (*top*),
19, 25, 26.

Front cover photograph by Still Pictures/Adrian Arbib

Printed in China

Contents

The words in **bold** in this book are explained in the glossary on page 31.

The power of music

For thousands of years, people have made music to entertain each other, to celebrate festivals and to praise their gods.

These schoolchildren in Ghana are clapping to the rhythm of drums.

All over the world, people tell old stories about the power of music.

An Ancient Greek myth tells how even the wild animals gathered around the musician, Orpheus, to hear him play his lyre.

A lyre has strings that you pluck with your fingers.

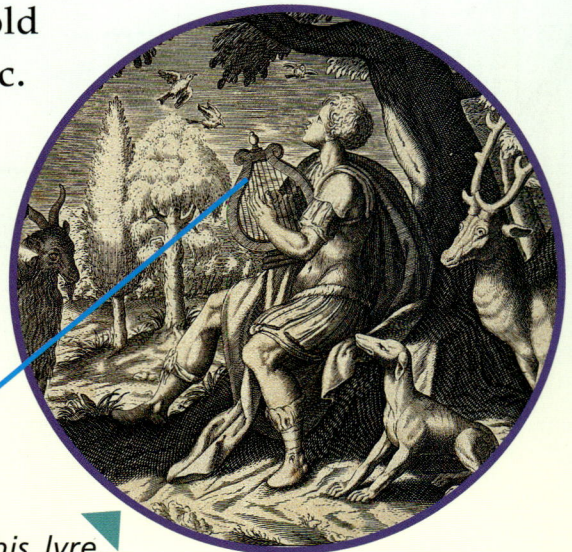

This old print shows Orpheus playing his lyre.

The first musical sounds were probably made
to send messages or signals to other people.

*Hunters signalled to each
other by blowing through
animal horns.*

*Warriors blew
trumpets to signal to their men
to go forward into battle.*

For hundreds of years, people living by the river
Congo, in West Africa, have sent messages from one
side of the river to the other with "talking drums".
The drummer beats the drums in patterns of high
and low notes. These echo the patterns of speech.

A large drum has a low note.   A small drum has a high note.

Play it!

We use different parts of our body to play different instruments.

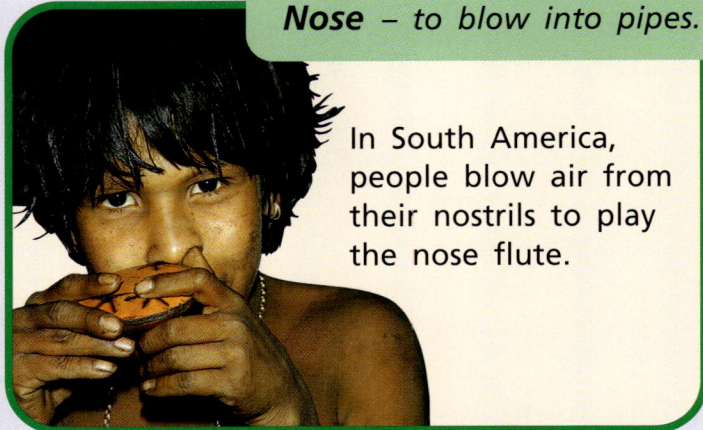

Nose – *to blow into pipes.*

In South America, people blow air from their nostrils to play the nose flute.

Feet – *to press keys and* **pedals**.

Most pianos have two pedals. The left pedal makes the sound softer. The right pedal makes the sound last longer. Some pianos have a third pedal which extends single notes.

Mouth – *to blow into instruments, or to blow across them.*

You have to make your mouth into a special shape to get the right sounds.

Arms, hands and fingers – *to hold instruments, to bang them, **pluck** strings, cover holes, and press down keys.*

On the violin, you press your fingers down on the strings to make different notes.

One-man-band

A one-man-band uses different parts of the body to play lots of instruments at the same time!

Hit it!

The first musical instruments were natural objects that made a sound when you hit them.

Hollow instruments

Hollow logs may have been the first drums.

These drums are made of hollow logs with skin stretched over one end.

This African plaque shows a man hitting the sides of drums made from hollow logs.

When a stick hits a hollow log it makes the log **vibrate**. The vibration goes into the air inside the log, making sound waves. The sound waves escape at either end.

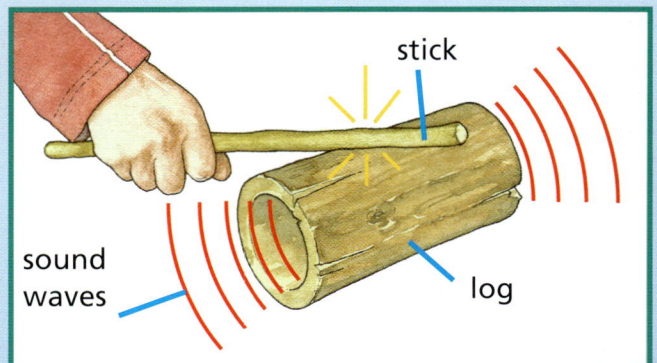

stick

sound waves

log

Thousands of years ago, people found that stretching an animal skin over the end of a hollow log made a drum that was much louder.

Some fruits, like the **gourd**, have a fleshy inside and a very hard skin. When the flesh is taken out, the hard skin makes a good small drum.

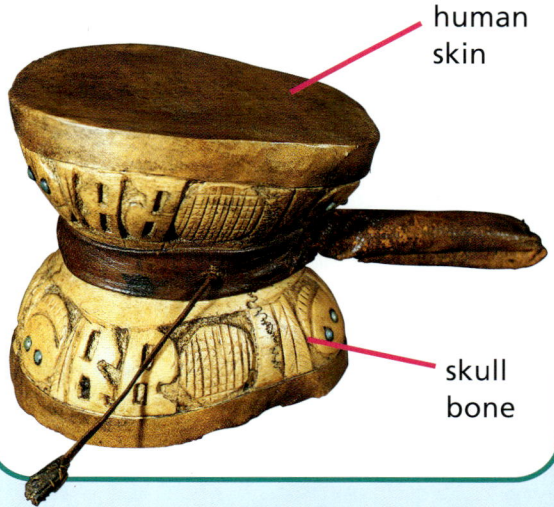

Today, plastic is stretched over drums, rather than animal skin.

Solid instruments

Hitting a solid block of wood also makes a sound. A smaller block makes a higher sound. A larger block makes a lower sound. When different sized blocks of wood are fixed together they make an instrument with lots of notes.

A marimba is an instrument traditionally made by the Zulu people in South Africa.

A marimba

It is made of blocks of wood, each one a different length. Hollow **gourds** are fixed to the blocks, to give louder and longer sounds.

This marimba is fixed on a wooden frame. Hollow vessels hang below to increase the sound.

A modern xylophone is made out of blocks of wood, like a marimba.

Metal

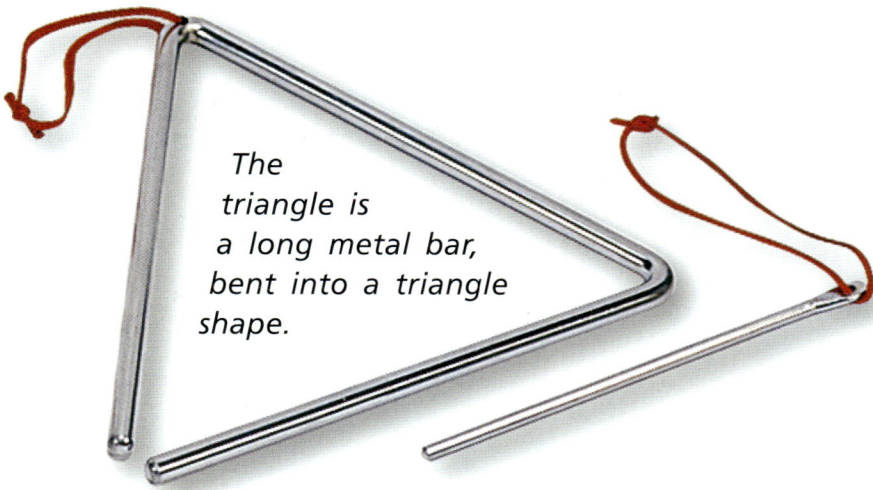

The triangle is a long metal bar, bent into a triangle shape.

When people first made metal, they found that metal bars made a good sound when hit.

Experiments with different metal shapes led to the making of gongs and bells.

In Java, and other islands in Indonesia, music is played on many different gongs.

Blow it!

Plants such as **reeds** and canes have tall hollow stems. When the wind blows across the tops of these stems, they make musical sounds.

How to make a wind instrument with bottles

1 Collect 10 glass bottles, all about the same size.

2 Put the bottles in a line.

3 Fill a jug with water.

4 Keep the first bottle empty (this will be the lowest note).

5 Put a little water into the second bottle.

6 Put more water into each bottle along the line, so that the last bottle is nearly full.

7 Blow across the top of each bottle to test the note.

8 **Tune** your bottles by adding or tipping out water, until they sound right.

9 Practise until you can play a tune, then amaze your family and friends!

The first wind instruments were pipes made of canes or hollow bones. The pipes were put in order of length.

The Ancient Greeks believed that when the wind whistled across the reeds, it was the god Pan, playing his pipes.

A flute player blows across a hole near the top of a metal tube. Along the tube are holes that the player can cover with his or her fingers. When different holes are covered, different notes are made.

Horns and trumpets

People discovered that you could also get a sound by blowing into something that was hollow, as well as by blowing across it.

They made a sound by putting their lips together at one end of it and blowing through, so their lips made the musical note. If the instrument was bigger at the other end, the sound was louder.

The shofar is one of the oldest instruments played today. It is a ram's horn played by Jewish people in religious ceremonies.

Sound gets stronger as the instrument gets wider.

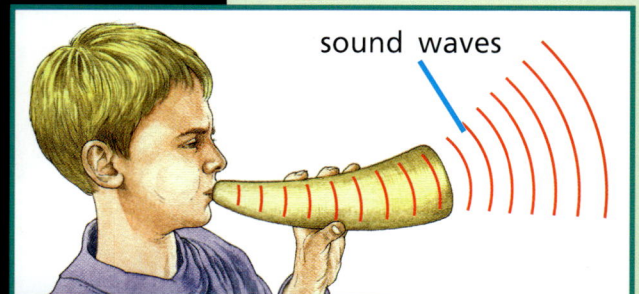

sound waves

When people first made metal, they copied the shape of animal horns to make metal horns or trumpets.

The month of Ramadan is very special for Muslims and there are festivals when it ends. The picture below, painted in 1237, shows the Eid festival at the end of Ramadan. Horn players and drummers are leading a procession.

Brass horns, drums, and flags mark the end of Ramadan.

Today, we have many different horns and trumpets. They are almost all made of metal, but we still talk about "horn players" in bands and **orchestras**.

trumpet

trombone

tuba

french
horn

Louis Armstrong (right) was an American jazz musician. Many people believe he was the best horn player of the 20th century.

Reed instruments

There is another way of making a sound by blowing.

Get two strips of thick paper. Hold them in your hands like this.

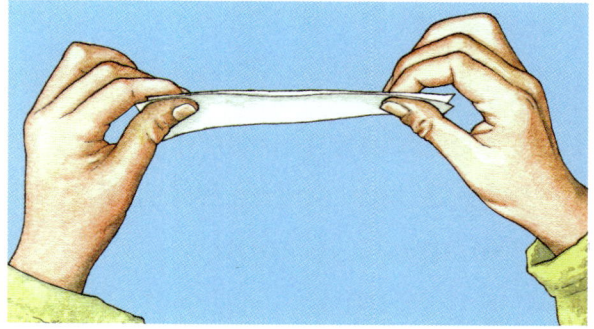

Put your lips very close to the middle of the papers and blow between them. Try twisting the papers a little. Keep blowing until the strips of paper **vibrate**, making a musical note.

People found that putting one or two small bits of **reed** into the top of a pipe made a rounder, fuller sound.

clasp to hold reed in place

reed

Many instruments have reeds in them today, such as this clarinet, the oboe, and saxophone.

Pluck it!

When people made bows and arrows, they found that **plucking** the string was a good way of testing if the string was tight.
It also made a good musical sound.

Hard straight objects can also be plucked. Try holding a ruler on the edge of a table and plucking ("pinging") it.

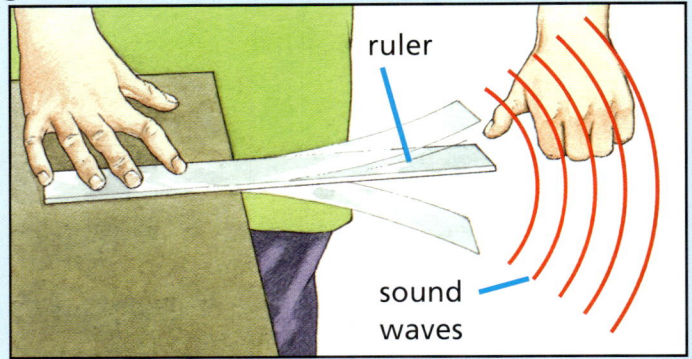

ruler

sound waves

The mbira, from South Africa, is carved from wood. The metal bars are flattened nails. You hold it in your hands and pluck the bars with your thumbs.

The mbira is also called the "thumb piano".

The first string instruments were sets of strings on simple wooden **frames** (like the one played by Orpheus, see page 4). The tighter the strings were stretched, the higher the note they made.

A harp's frame is designed to hold long strings at one end, and short strings at the other. The long strings make the low notes; the short strings make the high notes. The Bible tells us how, thousands of years ago, "David took a harp and played it" to King Saul.

A Celtic harp

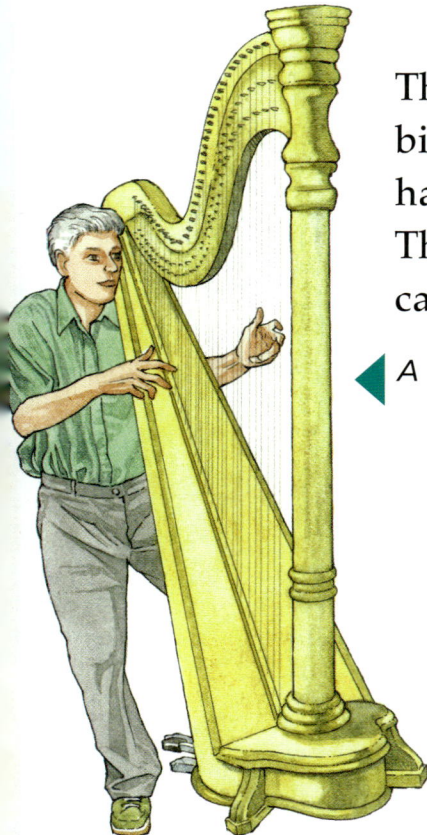

The modern harp is big, but in the past harps were smaller. They were easier to carry around.

A modern harp

A bell harp was small enough to carry and play while dancing.

People found that if you put a hollow **gourd** or box under the strings, the sound became louder and fuller. The same happened with instruments that you hit (see the marimba, page 10).

In China, the yueh-chin, or "moon-instrument", had four strings above a box shaped like a moon.

These street musicians are playing traditional Chinese instruments.

The yueh-chin. The strings are wound round pegs, so that they can be tightened or loosened to alter the note.

▲

About 1000 years ago, Arab musicians played an instrument called the "oot". This had lots of strings over a big hollow box. The player **plucked** the strings with their fingers or their fingernails.

The oot was copied by people in Europe. When it was made in England, its Arabic name "al oot" became "a lute".

This painting is from the 16th century. It was painted by Lorenzo Costa and is called A Concert. The lute is in the centre.

The lute became one of the most popular instruments in Europe. But from around 1600 more and more people played the guitar. A guitar was like a lute, but it was easier to hold and easier to play.

*A modern **acoustic** guitar*

six strings

a straight neck

body-shaped so it is easy to hold

pegs for tuning the strings

a hollow body

Guitars can be played with just the fingers, but some players use a **plectrum**. This small piece of hard material gives a clearer, sharper sound.

The invention of the **keyboard** made it easier to play lots of notes at the same time. Using all fingers, ten notes could be played at a time.

Most early keyboard instruments worked by **plucking** strings with a small piece of feather – the hard part called a "quill".

The spinet was a big harp put on its side, with a set of keys at the front. Each key worked a lever that pushed the quill against a string to pluck it.

This 18th-century painting, by Jonathan Richardson, shows a boy playing the spinet.

Based on the spinet, the piano was invented. In a piano, the strings are hit, not plucked.

Bow it!

A **plucked** string makes a short sound. You can make the note last longer by pulling another tight string (a **bow**) across the first string.

At first, people probably used the same bows they used to shoot arrows. Later, people made straight bows, with strings of long horse hair, just for playing instruments.

The Welsh crwth has six strings. Four strings are played with a bow, but the two strings on the left are plucked by the player's thumb.

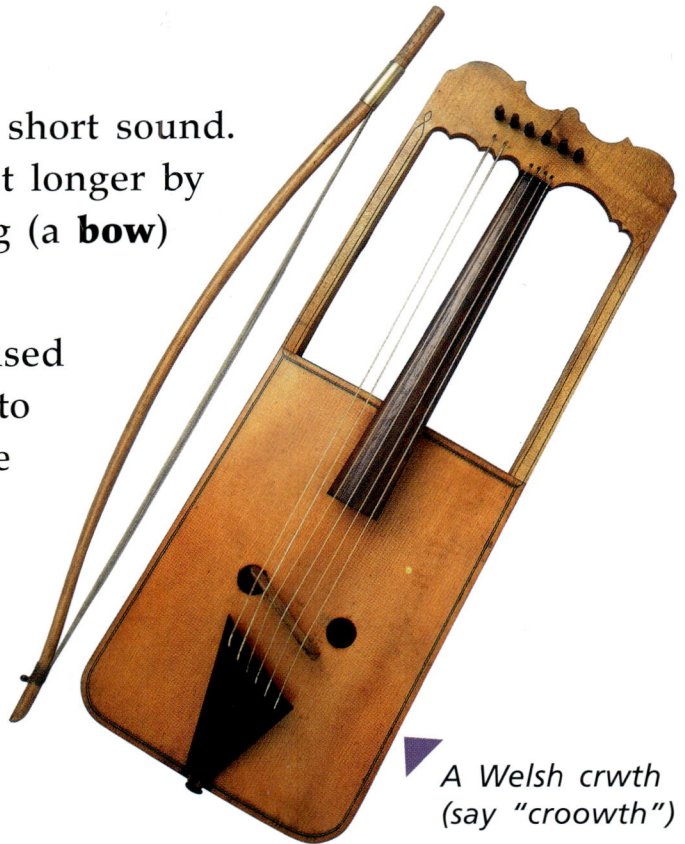

A Welsh crwth (say "croowth")

In an orchestra, there are usually more string instruments than any other kind of instrument.

All sorts of
instruments are
played with a bow.

A violin

A viola

A sordino
(pocket
violin)

A viola da
gamba (held
between the
legs)

A cello

A double
bass

Electrify it!

The first electrical instrument that became popular was the electric organ in the 1930s.

Ordinary organs were too big to move around, but an electric organ could be put in a van. Electric organs could be played loudly or softly by turning a control, just like on a TV or radio.

Soon, people started to electrify quiet instruments, like the guitar, so they could play loudly.

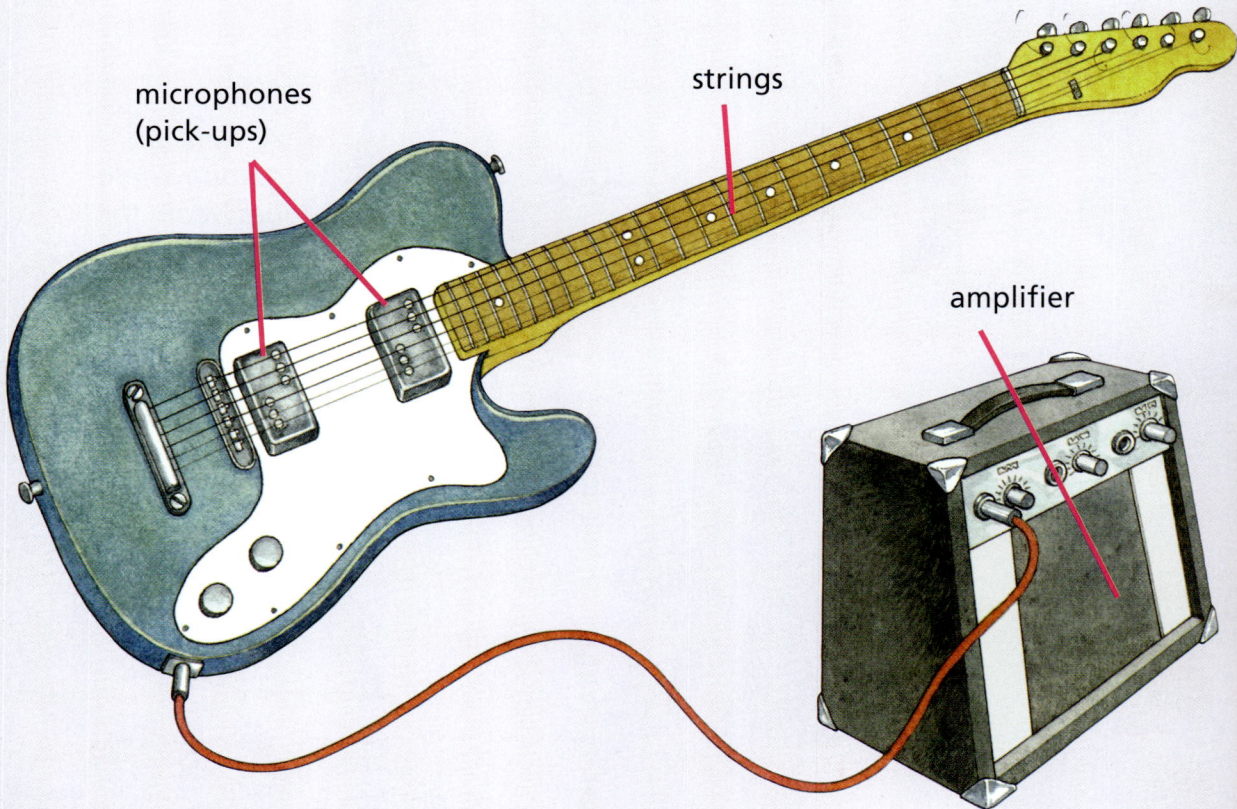

microphones
(pick-ups)

strings

amplifier

*Microphones on the electric guitar pick up the sound of the strings. The sound is then made louder by an **amplifier**.*

Ordinary **acoustic** stringed instruments are hollow to make the sound of the strings louder and better. But electric instruments can be all shapes and sizes, because it does not affect the sound they make.

Today, many instruments are electrified. You can get electric pianos, electric violins, electric drums, and electric guitars.

In the group Bond, *all the musicians perform with electric stringed instruments.*

In 1920, a Russian called Lev Theramin invented a new instrument. It was the first electrical instrument that made a sound that no other musical instrument could make. He called it a theramin.

A theramin is a tall metal rod sticking up out of a box of electronics. You play it by moving your hands around the rod. As your hands move, they change the magnetism around the rod; the changes are turned into sound.

Lev Theramin

Theramins have been used in music for space films and horror films. You can hear the strange "wee-oo-wee-oo" sound of a theramin in the music at the beginning of old episodes of Star Trek.

Sample it!

Computers are changing the way people make music.

Any sound can be recorded and put into a computer. The computer can make this **sample** sound higher, lower, longer or shorter.

If the sample is a sound from a trumpet, you can play a tune that sounds as if it is being played by a trumpeter.

Now one person can make the sound of a whole **orchestra**. Using samples of each instrument, a musician can build up a piece of music, recording each instrument in turn, then playing them all back together.

*Some schools have computers on which you can **compose** your own music.*

fantastic facts

The biggest drum is almost 4 metres across. It was played in London in 1987.

The highest price ever paid for a musical instrument is £902,000. It was paid in 1990 for an old violin.

£902,000

The quietest music was **composed** in 1952 by an American, John Cage. The piece is called "Four Minutes Thirty-three Seconds". It has no notes in it. The performer has to sit quietly, for four minutes and thirty-three seconds!

The largest crowd at a music concert was in 1983 at the US Festival in California, in the USA. There were 670,000 people listening.

The most notes played on the piano were played by Errol Garner. He could play more than 140 notes in one second!

Glossary

acoustic natural sound without electric amplifiers

amplifier object that makes the sound louder

bow piece of wood with hair or nylon stretched from one end to the other; pulled across strings to make them vibrate

compose to make a tune

frame piece or pieces of wood holding strings, bars or pipes

gourd fruit with a very hard skin, grown in Africa and Asia

keyboard set of wooden, plastic or metal blocks which can be pressed to make a note by plucking or hitting strings, or by working an electrical switch

orchestra lots of musicians playing together

pedal part of an instrument moved by the feet to change the sound

plectrum triangular piece of hard material (usually plastic) held in the fingers to pluck guitar strings

pluck to pull down a string or bar and suddenly let it go

reed plant growing in or near water, from which small pieces are cut to make the bits of wind instruments that make the sound

sample recorded sound which can be changed to any note and any length

tune (1) series of notes in a pattern to make music (2) to adjust an instrument to make the right note

vibrate to make something move very quickly from side to side or up and down

wind instrument musical instrument you blow into or across

Index